So ....ull Training Log and Diary

This Book Belongs To:

Cheyenne Simicak

Visit http://elegantnotebooks.com for more
sports training books.

Training Log and Diary
Nutrition Log and Diary
Strength and Conditioning Log and Diary

DATE: [   ] **WEEK:** [   ] **HOURS TRAINED:** [   ]

COACH: [   ] **TIME:** [   ]

GOALS

WARM UP/ DRILLS

TECHNIQUE 1

TECHNIQUE 2

NOTES

DATE:		WEEK:		HOURS TRAINED:	

COACH:		TIME:	

GOALS

WARM UP/ DRILLS

TECHNIQUE 1

TECHNIQUE 2

NOTES

DATE: _____ **WEEK:** _____ **HOURS TRAINED:** _____

COACH: _____ **TIME:** _____

GOALS

WARM UP/ DRILLS

TECHNIQUE 1

TECHNIQUE 2

NOTES

DATE: [   ] **WEEK:** [   ] **HOURS TRAINED:** [   ]

COACH: [   ] **TIME:** [   ]

GOALS

WARM UP/ DRILLS

TECHNIQUE 1

TECHNIQUE 2

NOTES

DATE: _____ **WEEK:** _____ **HOURS TRAINED:** _____

COACH: _____ **TIME:** _____

GOALS

WARM UP/ DRILLS

TECHNIQUE 1

TECHNIQUE 2

NOTES

DATE: **WEEK:**   **HOURS TRAINED:**

COACH: **TIME:**

GOALS

WARM UP/ DRILLS

TECHNIQUE 1

TECHNIQUE 2

NOTES

DATE: _____ **WEEK:** _____ **HOURS TRAINED:** _____

COACH: _____ **TIME:** _____

GOALS

WARM UP/ DRILLS

TECHNIQUE 1

TECHNIQUE 2

NOTES

DATE: _____ **WEEK:** _____ **HOURS TRAINED:** _____

COACH: _____ **TIME:** _____

GOALS

WARM UP/ DRILLS

TECHNIQUE 1

TECHNIQUE 2

NOTES

DATE: [   ]   **WEEK:** [   ]   **HOURS TRAINED:** [   ]

COACH: [   ]   **TIME:** [   ]

GOALS

WARM UP/ DRILLS

TECHNIQUE 1

TECHNIQUE 2

NOTES

DATE: WEEK: HOURS TRAINED:

COACH: TIME:

GOALS

WARM UP/ DRILLS

TECHNIQUE 1

TECHNIQUE 2

NOTES

DATE: _____ **WEEK:** _____ **HOURS TRAINED:** _____

COACH: _____ **TIME:** _____

GOALS

WARM UP/ DRILLS

TECHNIQUE 1

TECHNIQUE 2

NOTES

DATE: _____ **WEEK:** _____ **HOURS TRAINED:** _____

COACH: _____ **TIME:** _____

GOALS

WARM UP/ DRILLS

TECHNIQUE 1

TECHNIQUE 2

NOTES

DATE: **WEEK:** **HOURS TRAINED:**

COACH: **TIME:**

GOALS

WARM UP/ DRILLS

TECHNIQUE 1

TECHNIQUE 2

NOTES

DATE: [   ]   **WEEK:** [   ]   **HOURS TRAINED:** [   ]

COACH: [   ]   **TIME:** [   ]

GOALS

WARM UP/ DRILLS

TECHNIQUE 1

TECHNIQUE 2

NOTES

DATE: [ ]   **WEEK:** [ ]   **HOURS TRAINED:** [ ]

COACH: [ ]   **TIME:** [ ]

GOALS

WARM UP/ DRILLS

TECHNIQUE 1

TECHNIQUE 2

NOTES

DATE: | **WEEK:** | **HOURS TRAINED:**

COACH: | **TIME:**

GOALS

WARM UP/ DRILLS

TECHNIQUE 1

TECHNIQUE 2

NOTES

DATE: _____ **WEEK:** _____ **HOURS TRAINED:** _____

COACH: _____ **TIME:** _____

GOALS

WARM UP/ DRILLS

TECHNIQUE 1

TECHNIQUE 2

NOTES

DATE: **WEEK:**   **HOURS TRAINED:**

COACH: **TIME:**

GOALS

WARM UP/ DRILLS

TECHNIQUE 1

TECHNIQUE 2

NOTES

DATE: _____ **WEEK:** _____ **HOURS TRAINED:** _____

COACH: _____ **TIME:** _____

GOALS

WARM UP/ DRILLS

TECHNIQUE 1

TECHNIQUE 2

NOTES

DATE: | **WEEK:** | **HOURS TRAINED:**

COACH: | **TIME:**

GOALS

WARM UP/ DRILLS

TECHNIQUE 1

TECHNIQUE 2

NOTES

DATE: _____ **WEEK:** _____ **HOURS TRAINED:** _____

COACH: _____ **TIME:** _____

GOALS

WARM UP/ DRILLS

TECHNIQUE 1

TECHNIQUE 2

NOTES

DATE: _____ **WEEK:** _____ **HOURS TRAINED:** _____

COACH: _____ **TIME:** _____

GOALS

WARM UP/ DRILLS

TECHNIQUE 1

TECHNIQUE 2

NOTES

DATE: _____ **WEEK:** _____ **HOURS TRAINED:** _____

COACH: _____   **TIME:** _____

GOALS

WARM UP/ DRILLS

TECHNIQUE 1

TECHNIQUE 2

NOTES

DATE: _____ **WEEK:** _____ **HOURS TRAINED:** _____

COACH: _____ **TIME:** _____

GOALS

WARM UP/ DRILLS

TECHNIQUE 1

TECHNIQUE 2

NOTES

DATE: _____ **WEEK:** _____ **HOURS TRAINED:** _____

COACH: _____ **TIME:** _____

GOALS

WARM UP/ DRILLS

TECHNIQUE 1

TECHNIQUE 2

NOTES

DATE: **WEEK:**   **HOURS TRAINED:**

COACH: **TIME:**

GOALS

WARM UP/ DRILLS

TECHNIQUE 1

TECHNIQUE 2

NOTES

DATE: _____ **WEEK:** _____ **HOURS TRAINED:** _____

COACH: _____ **TIME:** _____

GOALS

WARM UP/ DRILLS

TECHNIQUE 1

TECHNIQUE 2

NOTES

DATE: **WEEK:**   **HOURS TRAINED:**

COACH: **TIME:**

GOALS

WARM UP/ DRILLS

TECHNIQUE 1

TECHNIQUE 2

NOTES

DATE: _____ **WEEK:** _____ **HOURS TRAINED:** _____

COACH: _____ **TIME:** _____

GOALS

WARM UP/ DRILLS

TECHNIQUE 1

TECHNIQUE 2

NOTES

DATE: _____ **WEEK:** _____ **HOURS TRAINED:** _____

COACH: _____ **TIME:** _____

GOALS

WARM UP/ DRILLS

TECHNIQUE 1

TECHNIQUE 2

NOTES

DATE: _____ **WEEK:** _____ **HOURS TRAINED:** _____

COACH: _____ **TIME:** _____

GOALS

WARM UP/ DRILLS

TECHNIQUE 1

TECHNIQUE 2

NOTES

DATE: _____ **WEEK:** _____ **HOURS TRAINED:** _____

COACH: _____ **TIME:** _____

GOALS

WARM UP/ DRILLS

TECHNIQUE 1

TECHNIQUE 2

NOTES

DATE: _____ **WEEK:** ___ **HOURS TRAINED:** _____

COACH: _____ **TIME:** _____

GOALS

WARM UP/ DRILLS

TECHNIQUE 1

TECHNIQUE 2

NOTES

DATE: **WEEK:**   **HOURS TRAINED:**

COACH: **TIME:**

GOALS

WARM UP/ DRILLS

TECHNIQUE 1

TECHNIQUE 2

NOTES

DATE: **WEEK:** **HOURS TRAINED:**

COACH: **TIME:**

GOALS

WARM UP/ DRILLS

TECHNIQUE 1

TECHNIQUE 2

NOTES

DATE: | **WEEK:** | **HOURS TRAINED:**

COACH: | **TIME:**

GOALS

WARM UP/ DRILLS

TECHNIQUE 1

TECHNIQUE 2

NOTES

DATE: _____ **WEEK:** _____ **HOURS TRAINED:** _____

COACH: _____ **TIME:** _____

GOALS

WARM UP/ DRILLS

TECHNIQUE 1

TECHNIQUE 2

NOTES

DATE: **WEEK:**   **HOURS TRAINED:**

COACH: **TIME:**

GOALS

WARM UP/ DRILLS

TECHNIQUE 1

TECHNIQUE 2

NOTES

DATE: **WEEK:**   **HOURS TRAINED:**

COACH: **TIME:**

GOALS

WARM UP/ DRILLS

TECHNIQUE 1

TECHNIQUE 2

NOTES

DATE: _____ **WEEK:** _____ **HOURS TRAINED:** _____

COACH: _____ **TIME:** _____

GOALS

WARM UP/ DRILLS

TECHNIQUE 1

TECHNIQUE 2

NOTES

DATE: [   ]   **WEEK:** [   ]   **HOURS TRAINED:** [   ]

COACH: [   ]   **TIME:** [   ]

GOALS

WARM UP/ DRILLS

TECHNIQUE 1

TECHNIQUE 2

NOTES

DATE: [_____] **WEEK:** [____] **HOURS TRAINED:** [_____]

COACH: [_____] **TIME:** [_____]

GOALS

WARM UP/ DRILLS

TECHNIQUE 1

TECHNIQUE 2

NOTES

DATE: _____ **WEEK:** _____ **HOURS TRAINED:** _____

COACH: _____ **TIME:** _____

GOALS

WARM UP/ DRILLS

TECHNIQUE 1

TECHNIQUE 2

NOTES

DATE: _____ **WEEK:** _____ **HOURS TRAINED:** _____

COACH: _____ **TIME:** _____

GOALS

WARM UP/ DRILLS

TECHNIQUE 1

TECHNIQUE 2

NOTES

DATE: **WEEK:**   **HOURS TRAINED:**

COACH: **TIME:**

GOALS

WARM UP/ DRILLS

TECHNIQUE 1

TECHNIQUE 2

NOTES

DATE: **WEEK:** **HOURS TRAINED:**

COACH: **TIME:**

GOALS

WARM UP/ DRILLS

TECHNIQUE 1

TECHNIQUE 2

NOTES

DATE: **WEEK:**   **HOURS TRAINED:**

COACH: **TIME:**

GOALS

WARM UP/ DRILLS

TECHNIQUE 1

TECHNIQUE 2

NOTES

DATE: [   ] **WEEK:** [   ] **HOURS TRAINED:** [   ]

COACH: [   ] **TIME:** [   ]

GOALS

WARM UP/ DRILLS

TECHNIQUE 1

TECHNIQUE 2

NOTES

DATE: _____ **WEEK:** ___ **HOURS TRAINED:** _____

COACH: _____ **TIME:** _____

GOALS

WARM UP/ DRILLS

TECHNIQUE 1

TECHNIQUE 2

NOTES

DATE: _____ **WEEK:** _____ **HOURS TRAINED:** _____

COACH: _____ **TIME:** _____

GOALS

WARM UP/ DRILLS

TECHNIQUE 1

TECHNIQUE 2

NOTES

DATE:		WEEK:		HOURS TRAINED:	

COACH:			TIME:	

GOALS

WARM UP/ DRILLS

TECHNIQUE 1

TECHNIQUE 2

NOTES

DATE: _____ **WEEK:** _____ **HOURS TRAINED:** _____

COACH: _____ **TIME:** _____

GOALS

WARM UP/ DRILLS

TECHNIQUE 1

TECHNIQUE 2

NOTES

DATE: **WEEK:**   **HOURS TRAINED:**

COACH: **TIME:**

GOALS

WARM UP/ DRILLS

TECHNIQUE 1

TECHNIQUE 2

NOTES

DATE: _____ **WEEK:** _____ **HOURS TRAINED:** _____

COACH: _____ **TIME:** _____

GOALS

WARM UP/ DRILLS

TECHNIQUE 1

TECHNIQUE 2

NOTES

DATE: _____ **WEEK:** _____ **HOURS TRAINED:** _____

COACH: _____ **TIME:** _____

GOALS

WARM UP/ DRILLS

TECHNIQUE 1

TECHNIQUE 2

NOTES

DATE: _____ **WEEK:** _____ **HOURS TRAINED:** _____

COACH: _____ **TIME:** _____

GOALS

WARM UP/ DRILLS

TECHNIQUE 1

TECHNIQUE 2

NOTES

DATE: _____ **WEEK:** _____ **HOURS TRAINED:** _____

COACH: _____ **TIME:** _____

GOALS

WARM UP/ DRILLS

TECHNIQUE 1

TECHNIQUE 2

NOTES

DATE: **WEEK:** **HOURS TRAINED:**

COACH: **TIME:**

GOALS

WARM UP/ DRILLS

TECHNIQUE 1

TECHNIQUE 2

NOTES

DATE: _____ **WEEK:** _____ **HOURS TRAINED:** _____

COACH: _____ **TIME:** _____

GOALS

WARM UP/ DRILLS

TECHNIQUE 1

TECHNIQUE 2

NOTES

DATE: **WEEK:** **HOURS TRAINED:**

COACH: **TIME:**

GOALS

WARM UP/ DRILLS

TECHNIQUE 1

TECHNIQUE 2

NOTES

DATE: _____ **WEEK:** _____ **HOURS TRAINED:** _____

COACH: _____ **TIME:** _____

GOALS

WARM UP/ DRILLS

TECHNIQUE 1

TECHNIQUE 2

NOTES

DATE: **WEEK:**   **HOURS TRAINED:**

COACH: **TIME:**

GOALS

WARM UP/ DRILLS

TECHNIQUE 1

TECHNIQUE 2

NOTES

DATE: _____ **WEEK:** _____ **HOURS TRAINED:** _____

COACH: _____ **TIME:** _____

GOALS

WARM UP/ DRILLS

TECHNIQUE 1

TECHNIQUE 2

NOTES

DATE: [_____] **WEEK:** [_____] **HOURS TRAINED:** [_____]

COACH: [_____] **TIME:** [_____]

GOALS

WARM UP/ DRILLS

TECHNIQUE 1

TECHNIQUE 2

NOTES

DATE: _____ **WEEK:** _____ **HOURS TRAINED:** _____

COACH: _____ **TIME:** _____

GOALS

WARM UP/ DRILLS

TECHNIQUE 1

TECHNIQUE 2

NOTES

DATE: [   ]   **WEEK:** [   ]   **HOURS TRAINED:** [   ]

COACH: [   ]   **TIME:** [   ]

GOALS

WARM UP/ DRILLS

TECHNIQUE 1

TECHNIQUE 2

NOTES

DATE: _____ **WEEK:** _____ **HOURS TRAINED:** _____

COACH: _____ **TIME:** _____

GOALS

WARM UP/ DRILLS

TECHNIQUE 1

TECHNIQUE 2

NOTES

DATE: [   ] **WEEK:** [   ] **HOURS TRAINED:** [   ]

COACH: [   ] **TIME:** [   ]

GOALS

WARM UP/ DRILLS

TECHNIQUE 1

TECHNIQUE 2

NOTES

DATE: _____ **WEEK:** _____ **HOURS TRAINED:** _____

COACH: _____ **TIME:** _____

GOALS

WARM UP/ DRILLS

TECHNIQUE 1

TECHNIQUE 2

NOTES

DATE: [   ] **WEEK:** [   ] **HOURS TRAINED:** [   ]

COACH: [   ] **TIME:** [   ]

GOALS

WARM UP/ DRILLS

TECHNIQUE 1

TECHNIQUE 2

NOTES

DATE: _____ **WEEK:** _____ **HOURS TRAINED:** _____

COACH: _____ **TIME:** _____

GOALS

WARM UP/ DRILLS

TECHNIQUE 1

TECHNIQUE 2

NOTES

DATE: **WEEK:**   **HOURS TRAINED:**

COACH: **TIME:**

GOALS

WARM UP/ DRILLS

TECHNIQUE 1

TECHNIQUE 2

NOTES

DATE: _____ **WEEK:** _____ **HOURS TRAINED:** _____

COACH: _____ **TIME:** _____

GOALS

WARM UP/ DRILLS

TECHNIQUE 1

TECHNIQUE 2

NOTES

DATE: [   ]   **WEEK:** [   ]   **HOURS TRAINED:** [   ]

COACH: [   ]   **TIME:** [   ]

GOALS

WARM UP/ DRILLS

TECHNIQUE 1

TECHNIQUE 2

NOTES

DATE: [ ] **WEEK:** [ ] **HOURS TRAINED:** [ ]

COACH: [ ] **TIME:** [ ]

GOALS

WARM UP/ DRILLS

TECHNIQUE 1

TECHNIQUE 2

NOTES

DATE: _____ **WEEK:** _____ **HOURS TRAINED:** _____

COACH: _____ **TIME:** _____

GOALS

WARM UP/ DRILLS

TECHNIQUE 1

TECHNIQUE 2

NOTES

DATE: **WEEK:** **HOURS TRAINED:**

COACH: **TIME:**

GOALS

WARM UP/ DRILLS

TECHNIQUE 1

TECHNIQUE 2

NOTES

DATE: **WEEK:**   **HOURS TRAINED:**

COACH: **TIME:**

GOALS

WARM UP/ DRILLS

TECHNIQUE 1

TECHNIQUE 2

NOTES

DATE: _____ **WEEK:** _____ **HOURS TRAINED:** _____

COACH: _____ **TIME:** _____

GOALS

WARM UP/ DRILLS

TECHNIQUE 1

TECHNIQUE 2

NOTES

DATE: **WEEK:**   **HOURS TRAINED:**

COACH: **TIME:**

GOALS

WARM UP/ DRILLS

TECHNIQUE 1

TECHNIQUE 2

NOTES

DATE: _____ **WEEK:** _____ **HOURS TRAINED:** _____

COACH: _____ **TIME:** _____

GOALS

WARM UP/ DRILLS

TECHNIQUE 1

TECHNIQUE 2

NOTES

DATE: _____ **WEEK:** _____ **HOURS TRAINED:** _____

COACH: _____ **TIME:** _____

GOALS

WARM UP/ DRILLS

TECHNIQUE 1

TECHNIQUE 2

NOTES

DATE: **WEEK:**   **HOURS TRAINED:**

COACH: **TIME:**

GOALS

WARM UP/ DRILLS

TECHNIQUE 1

TECHNIQUE 2

NOTES

DATE:		WEEK:		HOURS TRAINED:	

COACH:		TIME:	

GOALS

WARM UP/ DRILLS

TECHNIQUE 1

TECHNIQUE 2

NOTES

DATE: _____ **WEEK:** _____ **HOURS TRAINED:** _____

COACH: _____ **TIME:** _____

GOALS

WARM UP/ DRILLS

TECHNIQUE 1

TECHNIQUE 2

NOTES

DATE: _____   **WEEK:** _____   **HOURS TRAINED:** _____

COACH: _____   **TIME:** _____

GOALS

WARM UP/ DRILLS

TECHNIQUE 1

TECHNIQUE 2

NOTES

DATE: _____ **WEEK:** ___ **HOURS TRAINED:** _____

COACH: _____ **TIME:** _____

GOALS

WARM UP/ DRILLS

TECHNIQUE 1

TECHNIQUE 2

NOTES

DATE: [ ] **WEEK:** [ ] **HOURS TRAINED:** [ ]

COACH: [ ] **TIME:** [ ]

GOALS

WARM UP/ DRILLS

TECHNIQUE 1

TECHNIQUE 2

NOTES

DATE: _____   **WEEK:** _____   **HOURS TRAINED:** _____

COACH: _____   **TIME:** _____

GOALS

WARM UP/ DRILLS

TECHNIQUE 1

TECHNIQUE 2

NOTES

DATE: [   ] **WEEK:** [   ] **HOURS TRAINED:** [   ]

COACH: [   ] **TIME:** [   ]

GOALS

WARM UP/ DRILLS

TECHNIQUE 1

TECHNIQUE 2

NOTES

DATE: | **WEEK:** | **HOURS TRAINED:**

COACH: | **TIME:**

GOALS

WARM UP/ DRILLS

TECHNIQUE 1

TECHNIQUE 2

NOTES

DATE: [ ]   **WEEK:** [ ]   **HOURS TRAINED:** [ ]

COACH: [ ]   **TIME:** [ ]

GOALS

WARM UP/ DRILLS

TECHNIQUE 1

TECHNIQUE 2

NOTES

DATE: _____ **WEEK:** _____ **HOURS TRAINED:** _____

COACH: _____ **TIME:** _____

GOALS

WARM UP/ DRILLS

TECHNIQUE 1

TECHNIQUE 2

NOTES

DATE: _____   **WEEK:** _____   **HOURS TRAINED:** _____

COACH: _____   **TIME:** _____

GOALS

WARM UP/ DRILLS

TECHNIQUE 1

TECHNIQUE 2

NOTES

DATE: _____ **WEEK:** _____ **HOURS TRAINED:** _____

COACH: _____ **TIME:** _____

GOALS

WARM UP/ DRILLS

TECHNIQUE 1

TECHNIQUE 2

NOTES

DATE: _____ **WEEK:** _____ **HOURS TRAINED:** _____

COACH: _____ **TIME:** _____

GOALS

WARM UP/ DRILLS

TECHNIQUE 1

TECHNIQUE 2

NOTES

DATE: _____ **WEEK:** _____ **HOURS TRAINED:** _____

COACH: _____ **TIME:** _____

GOALS

WARM UP/ DRILLS

TECHNIQUE 1

TECHNIQUE 2

NOTES

DATE: _____ **WEEK:** _____ **HOURS TRAINED:** _____

COACH: _____ **TIME:** _____

GOALS

WARM UP/ DRILLS

TECHNIQUE 1

TECHNIQUE 2

NOTES

DATE: | **WEEK:** | **HOURS TRAINED:**

COACH: | **TIME:**

GOALS

WARM UP/ DRILLS

TECHNIQUE 1

TECHNIQUE 2

NOTES

DATE: _____ **WEEK:** _____ **HOURS TRAINED:** _____

COACH: _____ **TIME:** _____

GOALS

WARM UP/ DRILLS

TECHNIQUE 1

TECHNIQUE 2

NOTES

DATE: **WEEK:**   **HOURS TRAINED:**

COACH: **TIME:**

GOALS

WARM UP/ DRILLS

TECHNIQUE 1

TECHNIQUE 2

NOTES

DATE: [   ]   **WEEK:** [   ]   **HOURS TRAINED:** [   ]

COACH: [   ]   **TIME:** [   ]

GOALS

WARM UP/ DRILLS

TECHNIQUE 1

TECHNIQUE 2

NOTES

DATE: _____ **WEEK:** _____ **HOURS TRAINED:** _____

COACH: _____ **TIME:** _____

GOALS

WARM UP/ DRILLS

TECHNIQUE 1

TECHNIQUE 2

NOTES

DATE: **WEEK:** **HOURS TRAINED:**

COACH: **TIME:**

GOALS

WARM UP/ DRILLS

TECHNIQUE 1

TECHNIQUE 2

NOTES

DATE: _____ **WEEK:** _____ **HOURS TRAINED:** _____

COACH: _____ **TIME:** _____

GOALS

WARM UP/ DRILLS

TECHNIQUE 1

TECHNIQUE 2

NOTES

DATE: [ ] **WEEK:** [ ] **HOURS TRAINED:** [ ]

COACH: [ ] **TIME:** [ ]

GOALS

WARM UP/ DRILLS

TECHNIQUE 1

TECHNIQUE 2

NOTES

DATE: _____ **WEEK:** _____ **HOURS TRAINED:** _____

COACH: _____ **TIME:** _____

GOALS

WARM UP/ DRILLS

TECHNIQUE 1

TECHNIQUE 2

NOTES

DATE: _____ **WEEK:** ____ **HOURS TRAINED:** ____

COACH: _____ **TIME:** ____

GOALS

WARM UP/ DRILLS

TECHNIQUE 1

TECHNIQUE 2

NOTES

DATE: | **WEEK:** | **HOURS TRAINED:**

COACH: | **TIME:**

GOALS

WARM UP/ DRILLS

TECHNIQUE 1

TECHNIQUE 2

NOTES

DATE: **WEEK:**   **HOURS TRAINED:**

COACH: **TIME:**

GOALS

WARM UP/ DRILLS

TECHNIQUE 1

TECHNIQUE 2

NOTES

DATE: [   ] **WEEK:** [   ] **HOURS TRAINED:** [   ]

COACH: [   ] **TIME:** [   ]

GOALS

WARM UP/ DRILLS

TECHNIQUE 1

TECHNIQUE 2

NOTES

DATE: _____ **WEEK:** _____ **HOURS TRAINED:** _____

COACH: _____ **TIME:** _____

GOALS

WARM UP/ DRILLS

TECHNIQUE 1

TECHNIQUE 2

NOTES

DATE: _____ **WEEK:** _____ **HOURS TRAINED:** _____

COACH: _____ **TIME:** _____

GOALS

WARM UP/ DRILLS

TECHNIQUE 1

TECHNIQUE 2

NOTES

DATE: _____ **WEEK:** _____ **HOURS TRAINED:** _____

COACH: _____ **TIME:** _____

GOALS

WARM UP/ DRILLS

TECHNIQUE 1

TECHNIQUE 2

NOTES

DATE: **WEEK:**   **HOURS TRAINED:**

COACH: **TIME:**

GOALS

WARM UP/ DRILLS

TECHNIQUE 1

TECHNIQUE 2

NOTES

DATE: **WEEK:**   **HOURS TRAINED:**

COACH: **TIME:**

GOALS

WARM UP/ DRILLS

TECHNIQUE 1

TECHNIQUE 2

NOTES

DATE: _____ **WEEK:** _____ **HOURS TRAINED:** _____

COACH: _____ **TIME:** _____

GOALS

WARM UP/ DRILLS

TECHNIQUE 1

TECHNIQUE 2

NOTES

DATE: [   ]   **WEEK:** [   ]   **HOURS TRAINED:** [   ]

COACH: [   ]   **TIME:** [   ]

GOALS

WARM UP/ DRILLS

TECHNIQUE 1

TECHNIQUE 2

NOTES

DATE: | **WEEK:** | **HOURS TRAINED:**

COACH: | **TIME:**

GOALS

WARM UP/ DRILLS

TECHNIQUE 1

TECHNIQUE 2

NOTES

Manufactured by Amazon.ca
Bolton, ON